Contents

GW00394264

West Pier on a winter's day, see page 66

Introduction

R on Stuart was born in Birkenhead on Merseyside on March 7, 1918. His childhood, however, was spent both in the north and the south of England. His family lived in Worthing for four years and subsequently moved to a bungalow on Shoreham Beach, better known then as Bungalow Town.

Ron has fond memories of his early years and the adventurous life he enjoyed with his brother and two sisters in Bungalow Town. The children were always playing on the beach and often built rafts from driftwood that had been washed up on the shingle – and, of course, they went fishing, shrimping, winkling and beachcombing, as well as mushrooming with their mother in the fields near Shoreham Airport. Ron recalls that during the winter the waves were so high that often they covered the roof, and on particularly stormy nights the family had to seek refuge in the Church of the Good Shepherd across the road facing the beach. Unfortunately, the bungalow was wrecked during one of those stormy nights, which resulted in a family decision to return to Birkenhead.

Children of Bungalow Town

Children of the beach and sea,
Running wild, running free,
Free as the waves crashing on the shore,
Oh to be as free as that for evermore.
Those children of Bungalow Town,
Their faces, sun and wind blown brown.
Not for them school and paltry things,
Only the adventure of life, the joy it brings.
Homemade rafts made from driftwood found on the shore.
In the winter, the sea crashing over the bungalow, hear the roar.
Catching the fish and shrimps fresh from the sea,
Blackberrying for mother to make jam for our tea.
Covered in mud, picking winkles from the harbour sands.
Life was beautiful, life was in our eager hands.
Early morning dew, finding mushrooms in the long grass,
Why did these adventures have to pass?
Perhaps that's why I've retained those times and stowed away
Forever in my heart, to bring them out on a rainy day.

Ron left school when he was fourteen and moved to Hove with his family where he has lived since 1932. After various jobs an opportunity arose for him to become a seaside photographer on Hove seafront. His first camera was a Thornton-Pickard Reflex; however, most of his photographs were taken with

Smile Please!

Memories of Brighton seaside photographer Ron Stuart

*Ron on the lower promenade with his
first camera, a modification of the Thornton-
Pickard Reflex model, which was loaded
with 100 card negatives, c1949*

Edited by Madeleine Gentle

Day-trippers, see page 30

Dedication

To my late wife Phyllis and to my daughters
Sandra, Madeleine and Valerie

First published in 2003 by SB Publications
19 Grove Road, Seaford
East Sussex BN25 1TP
Tel: 01323 893498/fax 01323 893860
E-mail: sbpublications@tiscali.co.uk

ISBN 1 85770 271 9

A Photographer

The eye looks into the viewfinder,
The subject is there.
The user is the organ grinder,
Play it steady, take great care.
The finger presses, the shutter clicks,
Captures a moment of life,
Through the lens the moment flicks.
Like the blade of a knife,
The camera is a magic thing.
Records images for posterity,
The memories! The joy it can bring!
The photograph is for eternity.

Designed and typeset by
JEM Editorial@aol.com

Printed by
Pageturn Ltd
East Sussex, BN3 7EG
Tel: (01273) 821500

various models of Leica. Ron originally thought he would be too shy with the public but he soon found out that he was a natural. He recalls working on the promenade on September 3, 1939, when he heard a siren sounding. Everybody disappeared and he seemed to be the only person left on the seafront; World War Two had begun. Just a few months later, he volunteered for the RAF and served six years in the RAF Volunteer Reserve Service as a corporal on aircraft and general duties. He was stationed all over the

Ron with his mother, Rose, brother Eric and two sisters Elise and Violet outside their bungalow on Shoreham Beach, c1923

country and particularly recalls being at the RAF Air Crew Receiving Centre, Regent's Park, London, during the 'doodlebug summer' of 1944 and at the Harper Hill (Derbyshire) Bomb Dump where he worked on the transportation of bombs.

When Ron was demobbed in 1946 he returned to his job as a photographer on the seafront. During the winter he commuted to London and worked at various department stores including Gamages (then one of the largest stores in London) taking photographs of children with Father Christmas, and he also completed fifteen seasons at the fairground of the Bertram Mills Circus at Olympia. He used props for his photographs – a pink elephant and a stuffed donkey – as 'gimmicks'. Everyday, at Olympia, a celebrity could be spotted and in consequence Ron built up a fine collection of snapshots of the famous, including those of Eartha Kitt, Eamonn Andrews, Prince Charles and Coco the Clown.

Before retiring in the early 1980s Ron worked for ten seasons at Allders in Portsmouth where he was the resident photographer in the Father Christmas Grotto.

Ron's favourite spot as a seaside photographer was without doubt the Palace Pier forecourt. He worked there during the spring and summer seasons for many years. He used fake animal props made from *papier maché* which, supposedly, were made by local art students, as well as two real parrots, Sputnik and Jacko. He has taken

Ron at work on the Palace Pier forecourt nursing Sputnik the parrot, c 1960.

thousands of photographs, many of which have been sent around the world. As he says: 'People from all over the planet visit Brighton.'

Since Ron's retirement his photographic collection has attracted the attention of both print and broadcast journalists. In 1995 the *Daily Mail* featured a centre spread showing examples of his work that included pictures of such celebrities as Rex Harrison, Kay Kendall and David Frost. There followed features in the *The Argus* and *Brighton & Hove Leader* and interviews on local television and Radio 4.

In 1999, Ron won a top award with his early 1950s' day-trippers' photograph of two old women. Ron had entered this in the 'Photos For the Future' competition, which was sponsored by the History Channel and by *The Express*. There were 6,000 entries and Ron was thrilled to receive one of five top awards. In addition, two of his photographs depicting fishermen pulling in their nets appeared in an exhibition at the Brighton Fishing Museum on the lower promenade when it opened in 1995. In the same year Ron was chosen as one of 'The 100 Faces of Brighton & Hove' – by Brighton and Hove Council in conjunction with *The Argus*, as part of the promotion for city status.

Ron is also proud of the fact that some of his photographs are being shown as a permanent feature in the History of Brighton and Hove Exhibition at the newly refurbished Brighton Museum.

Another string to Ron's bow is that he is an accomplished artist and poet; some of his poems are contained in this book to complement his photographs. His poetry has also been published in this country

Ron Stuart and Norman Wisdom on the lower promenade; Norman was appearing at the Hippodrome Theatre, c1958

and in Canada. Utilising his writing skills again, he became a voluntary contributor between 1986 and 1991 for The Tom Harrisson Mass-Observation Archive run by Sussex University.

Ron believes that he chose the right path in life as a photographer. As he says: 'A photograph is a moment in somebody's life.' He likes to think of his photographs on mantel-shelves, walls and in family albums and he knows that someone somewhere is saying – 'that was your Gran and Grandad on honeymoon in Brighton'; a special memory caught on camera forever.

The two parrots, Sputnik and Jacko, taking a rest between photographs

Madeleine Gentle
Brighton, 2003

Brighton and Hove

This jewel shines on the coast,
This town that's got the most,
Full of colour and zest,
It's got to be the best.
This is the place to be,
This place down by the sea,
Brighton and Hove known world wide.
Our people are so full of pride
For its culture and history,
For its vigour and vitality,
A city it has got to be,
Our bubbling town, down by the sea.

Stars of stage and screen

Max Miller (*c*1948): Max was one of Britain's greatest variety show comedians; a master of timing and double entendre. I met him in the bar of Clarges Hotel, Marine Parade, on the seafront. He lived quite close to this hotel in Burlington Street. 'Can I take a photograph of you, Max?' I said. He replied, 'Okay Ron, take me with the bird.'

Magnificent Max

Roars of laughter come from the hippodrome,
The Cheekie Chappie is playing at home.
'Now, now, lady, don't get shirty,
You're lookin' clean but laughin' dirty'.
The innuendoes come fast and slick,
The master doesn't miss a trick.
Out of a pocket comes the little blue book,
Then a smile by Max and a saucy look,
The flamboyant suit, the kipper tie,
The naughty glint that's in his eye.
It's not so hard to understand
Why he holds the audience in his hand.
The spotlight on the cheeky smile,
The tilted hat, has he got style?
'I fell in love with Mary from the dairy',
Then the little dance, also necessary
As part of one of the greatest acts,
The wonderful comic, magnificent Max.
There'll never be another, he is the one,
He'll always be Brighton's favourite son.

James Mason (*c*1960): 'I say, old boy, would you mind awfully taking our photograph with the parrot?' I was aware of the distinctive voice and who it was. Before I looked up, of course, I was right – it was James Mason, a leading British film actor with a rich, mellow voice, who had taken up a pose by the stuffed animal on the Palace Pier forecourt. He paid me for the photograph and gave me the address of where he wanted it sent. He then said: 'Thank you so much. Would you be kind enough now to tell me where we can get a nice pot of tea?' He shook me by the hand and then made for 'Ye Olde Bun Shoppe' in Pool Valley.

Stars of stage and screen

Robert Morley (*c*1957): The famous British stage and film character actor, writer and wit, was looking disappointedly at the board outside the coach office on the Palace Pier forecourt. He had just missed the coach to Wye races. He said to me: 'Never mind, I shall go to the pier and sit in a deckchair'. About half an hour later I took a photograph of two dear old ladies. I mentioned that Robert Morley was on the pier. They got excited at hearing this; he must have been a favourite of theirs. An hour later they strolled off the pier. 'Did you see him?', I asked. 'Oh yes', said one. 'He was asleep in a deckchair. We woke him up.' 'What did he say?' I said. 'Charming!' she said. When Robert eventually left the pier, he kind of gave me a funny look!

Sir Ralph Richardson (*c*1963): I photographed the eminent British character actor of stage and screen on the Palace Pier forecourt admiring the parrots. He was unaware that I had taken the photograph. A couple of days later I took a print to the stage door of the Theatre Royal where he was appearing. I told the doorman: 'Give this to Sir Ralph and don't say anything'. The next morning he appeared at the Palace Pier with another gentleman and said: 'Laddie, thank you for your wonderful photo. We had the photographers down from London yesterday taking shots of us prior to going to the West End. I told them the best photographer in the country is down at the Palace Pier'.

Naturally, I took his kind comment with a pinch of salt, but what a nice gesture on the part of the perfect gentleman. He then asked me to take his friend and himself with the parrots. He remarked that he had a parrot as a pet and sometimes when he went for a drive in his car, the parrot sat on his shoulder.

Stars of stage and screen

Margaret Rutherford (*c*1961): A taxi pulled up opposite the Palace Pier and out stepped Margaret Rutherford, the delightfully eccentric British actress (mostly comedy), with her husband, actor Stringer Davis, who usually played small roles in her films. The couple made straight for my stand and Margaret said: 'We must have a photograph with the parrot', and I duly obliged. Margaret Rutherford was made a Dame in 1966.

Rex Harrison and Kay Kendall (*c*1958): I caught this good-looking British couple, Rex Harrison and Kay Kendall, in this impromptu shot, strolling on the lower promenade. Rex had many starring roles during his acting career including his brilliant performance in *My Fair Lady* as Professor Higgins. Kay, best remembered for her leading role in *Genevieve*, the classic film based on the Veteran Car Run from London to Brighton, died from leukaemia in 1959 aged thirty-two.

Stars of stage and screen

Kenneth Williams (*c*1963): Kenneth is seen here with Peter Butterworth, Janet Brown and their children on the Palace Pier forecourt. Kenneth asked me to take this photograph with his friends and their children and, of course, the parrot. They had come down to Brighton for the day. He ordered half a dozen prints and insisted that he paid for them. This photograph appears in Faith Brown's autobiography.

Norman Wisdom (*c*1958): British film comic Norman Wisdom is seated on one of my props on the lower promenade. He was appearing at the Hippodrome Theatre in that year's summer show. The theatre closed in 1965 and is now a bingo hall.

Norman began his career in variety shows but is perhaps best known for his slapstick, cloth-capped comedy film roles in the early 1950s. I believe that I have captured an example of his comic genius.

Dame Flora Robson (*c*1973): The distinguished British actress was photographed on the lower promenade with her sister Sheila and an actor friend. She was a regular visitor to Brighton and often asked to have her photograph taken. She called me 'her brown photographer', which I assume was because of my suntan. Dame Flora retired to Brighton in the 1970s.

Stars of stage and screen

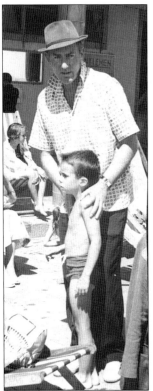

Michael Wilding (*c*1956), left: British actor, Michael Wilding and his son on the lower promenade by the West Pier. At the time he was married to Elizabeth Taylor. He was a big box office star with Anna Neagle in a post-war series of comedies.

Melvyn Hayes (*c*1975), right: British comedy character actor, Melvyn Hayes, on the lower promenade when he was down for the day. He started acting on stage during adolescence but I can remember seeing him in the films *The Young Ones* and *Summer Holiday* with Cliff Richard and, course, on television in *It Ain't Half Hot, Mum*.

Terry Thomas (*c*1973), below right: British film actor, Terry Thomas, famous for his upper-crust, exaggerated accent, was staying with his family, who were on holiday at the time, at the Metropole Hotel, which can be seen in the background.

Dawn Addams (*c*1955), left: British-born film actress, Dawn Addams, with her dogs on the Palace Pier forecourt. Dawn lived in Hove at the time. She appeared as a 'glam-our girl' in some Hollywood films during the 1950s, and was a familiar sight walking her dogs on the seafront.

Stars of stage and screen

Dennis Price (*c*1950): British film actor, Dennis Price, was pacing up and down on the Palace Pier forecourt one morning when I asked him if I could take his photograph. He said, 'By all means, when my wife and daughter arrive'. Many of Dennis's roles were of playing smooth, devious-looking, aristocratic charmers.

Sir John Gielgud (*c*1965) below: British stage and film actor, John Gielgud, with a friend, walking off the Palace Pier. He was an actor of great distinction who played a number of Shakespearian roles. He was appearing at the Theatre Royal.

Kenneth Moore (*c*1969), right: Prior to this photograph being taken on the forecourt of the Palace Pier, the British film actor Kenneth Moore had booked a trip at the coach office to the Sussex countryside for himself and his daughter. He burst into stardom in 1953 when he had a leading role in the film *Genevieve* with Kay Kendall.

Stars of stage and screen

Eric Portman (*c*1958): British film actor, Eric Portman, taking a relaxing stroll on the lower promenade.

Gladys Cooper (*c*1967): Photographed on the Palace Pier forecourt. She was extremely fond of Brighton and was a regular visitor. On this occasion, she brought these two children to Brighton for a day out; they appeared to be her grandchildren. She was a distinguished British stage and film actress.

Sid James (*c*1959): British comedy actor, Sid James, on the lower promenade, when filming in Brighton. Sid was, of course, famous for his roles in the radio and television comedy series *Hancock's Half Hour* and the Carry On films that were made between 1958 and 1980.

Stars of stage and screen

Ray Brooks (*c*1969): British film actor, Ray Brooks, with his child on the Palace Pier forecourt. Ray was a local boy and his parents worked on the buses. He played many leading roles on television and one of his best-known films was *The Knack*, a comedy farce which also starred Michael Crawford and Rita Tushingham.

Sheila Hancock (*c*1968): British stage and television actress, Sheila Hancock, with her daughter Melanie from her first marriage to Alec Ross on the Palace Pier forecourt. In 1973 Sheila married John Thaw, best remembered for *Morse*, who died from cancer in 2002.

Stars of stage and screen

Tony Curtis and Roger Moore (*c*1972): American actor, Tony Curtis, and British actor, Roger Moore, filming for an episode of the 1971–1972 television series *The Persuaders* near the Palace Pier. Between takes, they conversed freely with the onlookers. Roger is best known as 007 in seven James Bond films made between 1973 and 1985. And let's not forget Tony's superb performance in *Some Like it Hot*.

Stars of stage and screen

Jess Conrad and **Aliki** (*c*1965): Jess Conrad and Aliki were taken to Rottingdean to be photographed for the promotion of the première of a film that was held at the Essoldo cinema. The media called Aliki 'the Greek Brigitte Bardot'. Jess, of course, was a well-known pop star of the 1960s.

Michael Dennison and **Dulcie Gray** (*c*1949): This popular post-war British stage and screen couple, Michael Dennison and Dulcie Gray, strolling past the Palace Pier on a Sunday morning. They were appearing at the Theatre Royal.

Sir Alec Guinness (*c*1970): This is an impromptu shot of British actor, Sir Alec Guinness, on the Palace Pier forecourt. I can remember him appearing at the Palace Pier Theatre a few years after the war. Whenever Sir Alec appeared at the Theatre Royal he always spent a lot of time on the pier because of his love of repertory theatre. He was an extremely distinguished actor and had many leading roles; in fact, he was awarded an Oscar for his role in *The Bridge on the River Kwai*.

Stars of stage and screen

Anthea Askey and Freddie Mills (*c*1959): The former British boxer, Freddie Mills, and Anthea Askey, seen on the lower promenade. They were appearing in summer show at the Hippodrome Theatre and were both in a 'larking about' mood! Anthea was versatile like her father Arthur (right); as well as being an excellent comedienne, she was also a good singer.

Paul Massie (*c*1968): Canadian actor Paul Massie taking an early morning stroll on the Palace Pier. He was appearing at the Theatre Royal. Paul was often confused with Daniel Massey, the actor son of that other Canadian actor, Raymond Massey.

Arthur Askey (*c*1958): British comic, Arthur Askey, on the Palace Pier forecourt. He appeared in many variety shows, on radio and in pantomime in the course of his career, and was a master of the ad lib. He was one of the many great comedians from Liverpool. He used to perform by skipping around the stage and incorporating an energetic song and dance routine into his act.

Stars of stage and screen

Peter Bull (*c*1955): British film actor, Peter Bull, strolling on the lower promenade, was a well-known supporting actor in many British films.

Cesar Romero (*c*1950): Handsome Italian-Mexican film actor, Cesar Romero, taking a stroll on the Palace Pier on a visit to Britain; he was a big Hollywood star.

Tommy Trinder and **Eddie Gray** (*c*1969): British variety show comedians, Tommy Trinder and Eddie Gray, on the forecourt when they were appearing in the summer show at the Palace Pier Theatre, which unfortunately closed down in 1973. I used to see Tommy quite often during the summer season; we talked a lot about football and, of course, at that time he was the chairman of Fulham Football Club.

Stars of stage and screen

Douglass Montgomery (*c*1950): Leading Canadian actor, Douglass Montgomery, with a companion on the Palace Pier forecourt. He was popular on the radio during World War II while serving with the Canadian army. He also made several films including *The Way to the Stars* but was not seen after the mid-1950s. He was with a group of friends when this photograph was taken and everybody laughed when he suddenly leapt over the pier turnstile!

Musicians, singers and pop stars

Malcolm Roberts (*c*1969): British ballad singer, Malcolm Roberts, who was a pop star in the late 1960s, on the Palace Pier forecourt. He was appearing in the Ronnie Corbett summer show at the Palace Pier Theatre. He had three hit singles that entered the charts between 1967 and 1969, including the popular Love is All which was a great success at the Rio Song Festival. He appeared in cabaret and on television in this country and all over the world. His latter years were, however, spent concentrating on song-writing and production. He died recently aged fifty-eight.

Max Bygraves (*c*1955): Max Bygraves playing the barrel organ for charity (taken from the upper promenade). He was starring in the summer show at the Hippodrome Theatre. I had the pleasure of meeting most of his family including his mum and dad.

Musicians, singers and pop stars

Billy J Kramer (*c*1964): Pop star Billy J Kramer (of Billy J Kramer and the Dakotas) was appearing at the *Melody Maker* pop star award ceremony at the Regent Ballroom. His group were voted the best newcomers of 1963; just one of the many pop stars emerging from Liverpool during this era.

Long John Baldry (*c*1968): Legendary British blues singer Long John Baldry, on the Palace Pier forecourt, was in Brighton for a concert. He was called 'Long' John because of his height of 6ft 7in.

Ruby Murray (*c*1958): The popular Irish singing sensation was a household name in the mid-1950s. She is seen here in a bar on the lower promenade when she was accompanied by a party of friends. During the 1950s Ruby had five singles in the Top 20 at the same time. Perhaps the best-known was Softly, Softly.

Musicians, singers and pop stars

Sam Costa (*c1965*): Sam Costa with his wife on the Palace Pier forecourt. He appeared in the popular radio show *Much-Binding-in-the-Marsh* from the mid-1940s to the mid-1950s. He had a great voice and was one of the big band singers of the era. He was also a DJ on Radio Luxembourg in the 1960s and was known as one of the 'dads' of the DJs because of his personality and record knowledge, which made him popular with young and old alike.

George Formby (*c1952*): Popular singing comedian George Formby with his little dog on the lower promenade during one of his frequent visits to Brighton. We often used to pass the time of day and one day I remarked: 'What a great little dog you have'. He replied: 'The trouble is he finds girlfriends, loves them and then leaves them!' George appeared in many variety shows playing his ukulele, especially during the music hall days between 1920 and 1960.

Musicians, singers and pop stars

Donald Peers (c1957): Donald Peers leaning against a montage of my photographs on display on the lower promenade. He moved to Hove around this time and I suppose it could be said that he was a forerunner of the pop star and was variety's number one singing star of the 1950s. He was the first singer in this country to perform in front of the 'screaming bobby-soxers'. His recording of In A Shady Nook (By A Babbling Brook) in 1944 became his lifelong theme tune.

Victor Borge (c1972): Danish-born Victor Borge, a brilliant comedian and pianist, on the Palance Pier forecourt. He was in Brighton performing in concert at the Dome Theatre with his one-man show. For many years he was an international television and stage favourite. He loved performing in Brighton as he found that the audience always gave him such a warm reception.

Television personalities

Gilbert Harding (*c*1952), left, of *What's My Line?* fame, taking a stroll on the lower promenade. He was one of Brighton's most famous residents at the time; he lived in Montpelier Villas.

David Frost (*c*1968): A young David Frost leaning against a stuffed animal on the Palace Pier forecourt. At this time, he had already established himself as a well-known television personality in *That Was The Week That Was* in 1962–1963.

Dick Emery (*c*1970): Comic Dick Emery is seen here on the Palace Pier forecourt where he was promoting this three-wheeled car. He was appearing in the summer show at the Palace Pier Theatre. He had a great interest in cars and was also a trained pilot.

Television personalities

Mike Yarwood (*c*1963): Impressionist Mike Yarwood with a friend on the Palace Pier forecourt. He was at the peak of his career and was appearing at the Hippodrome Theatre. He can be best remembered for his impersonations of the late Harold Wilson, the Labour Party Prime Minister, and of Conservative Party Prime Minister Edward Heath, as well as of Brian Clough (below).

Brian Clough (*c*1960): Brian Clough on the West Street upper promenade; he was a famous footballer, playing for Middlesborough at the time. He was in Brighton with his club, prior to playing in a big match in London. He was the manager of the Brighton and Hove Albion Football Club for the season 1973–1974. He became one of football's most successful managers, especially during his time with Nottingham Forest. He was extremely outspoken and didn't suffer fools gladly.

Television personalities

Jimmy Savile (*c*1970): Jimmy Savile walking past the Palace Pier during one of his many charity walks. He has raised thousands of pounds for charity as well as being a volunteer worker in various hospitals. He was a familiar face on television and radio during the 1960s, 1970s and 1980s and is best known for his presentation of *Top of the Pops* and *Jim'll Fix It*.

Politicians

Lord Hailsham (*c*1961): Lord Hailsham (Quintin Hogg) was in Brighton for the Tory Party Conference. 'I'm being hounded by the press,' he told me, but I think he was enjoying the attention! The press photographers asked me if they could borrow the parrot for a publicity shot of Lord Hailsham. I duly gave them the bird. The photograph appeared in the London evening papers. Lord Hailsham relinquished his peerage in 1963 as he wanted to continue as MP for Marylebone.

Chris Chataway (*c*1961): Chris and a colleague strolling past the Odeon cinema in West Street on their way to the Tory Party Conference. He was MP for Lewisham North (1959–1966) and for Chichester (1969–1974). The person in the background was the manager of the cinema. Chris is perhaps best known for his athletic championship performances in 1954 in the European and Empire Games, when he won silver and gold medals respectively.

Politicians

Cyril Smith (*c*1973): The genial politician, affectionately known as 'Big Cyril' in his home town of Rochdale, strolling on the lower promenade when he was attending the Liberal Party Conference. He was well respected for his tireless work in his constituency and for his support of the underdog; indeed a people's champion. He was awarded the MBE in 1966 and was knighted in 1988, the same year that he announced his retirement as an MP.

Ian Mikado and **Aneurin Bevan** (*c*1957): Ian Mikado and Aneurin Bevan on the lower promenade, opposite West Street, when they were attending the Labour Party Conference in Brighton. Ian was an MP for Reading in the 1950s and Aneurin was MP for Ebbw Vale from 1929 until he died.

Day-trippers

Two dear ladies (*c*1957): These 'two dear ladies' were dancing a jig on the Palace Pier forecourt and were characteristic of typical day-trippers during the 1950s. I think the photo caught their joy and 'out-for-the-day' pleasure. This photo won a top award in the Photos For the Future competition in 1999 that was sponsored by the History Channel on Channel 4 TV and *The Express*.

Day-trippers

Hippies and beatniks (*c*1965): A colony of hippies and beatniks arrived on the beach opposite the fish market and some of them waded into the water fully clothed!

A group of day-trippers (*c*1970): These disabled people on the Palace Pier forecourt were 'down for the day'.

Day-trippers

Feeding time! (*c*1968): A couple of happy day-trippers were having fun trying to feed the stuffed animal with candy floss on the Palace Pier forecourt.

Pearly King, Queen and Princess (*c*1958): I used to love these colourful characters from London; the Pearly King, Queen and Princess. They visited Brighton every summer. You can see the pleasure on the onlookers' faces standing behind them on the Palace Pier forecourt.

Day-trippers

Chelsea Pensioners (*c*1965): These wonderful Chelsea Pensioners from London, pictured here on the Palace Pier forecourt, visited Brighton every year and were always made welcome by residents and holidaymakers alike.

A couple of trendy girls (*c*1975): These girls in their bell-bottoms posed for me on the lower promenade between the two piers; they were obviously enjoying their day out.

Smile please! (*c*1965): This little girl wasn't quite sure whether she was enjoying her day out; she wouldn't smile for me. Note the cost of passport photographs advertised in the kiosk on the Palace Pier forecourt!

Day-trippers

Mods and Rockers (1964): Images of the notorious clash between the Mods and Rockers at Brighton on the May Bank Holiday Monday of 1964. There was a pitched battle on the Aquarium terrace with flying deckchairs being used as missiles. Police joined the melée and they can be distinguished by their white helmets in the picture above. Police on horseback on the pier forecourt had never been seen before. People couldn't get on or off the pier because of the sheer volume of the crowds.

Day-trippers

The photograph on the right shows the arrival of the Black Maria. The group photograph of Rockers below is part of the local history exhibition at Brighton Museum.

(Mods rode motor-scooters and liked pop music, smart clothes and dancing; Rockers were motorcyclists who wore studded leather clothing and liked heavy rock music.)

Day-trippers

Me and My Old Dutch (*c*1965): This couple from London, whom I nicknamed 'Me and My Old Dutch', visited Brighton every year and had their photograph taken on the Palace Pier.

'I ain't got no body!' (*c*1961): I'll always remember taking these shots on the beach adjacent to the Palace Pier. The young boy had such a happy disposition. The onlookers, however, were somewhat bemused!

Happy trio (*c*1965): Children as well as adults enjoyed being photographed with the parrot on the Palace Pier forecourt.

The Veteran Car Run (*c*1995): Thousands turn out to see the 'old crocks' run from London to Brighton each year. Here one approaches the finish line. See page 57 for more pictures.

Palace Pier (1999): I was out for a stroll one warm, sunny day and could not resist taking this photo (above) of the Palace Pier; so vibrant, full of day-trippers, holidaymakers and local residents alike. The name was changed from the Palace Pier to Brighton Pier (picture left) in 2000; allegedly a marketing decision.

Brighton and Hove Albion Football Club (1978): Above, the Seagulls leaving the Goldstone Ground in an open-decker bus for a parade through the streets in honour of their promotion to Division 1. Below (2002), the Seagulls celebrate once more with a parade celebrating promotion to Division 1 – and being Division 2 Champions. See also pages 59 and 60.

Carousel and stalls (1995): Lower promenade view between the two piers on the day when the Brighton Fishing Museum opened.

Brighton Sea Cadets (1996): The cadets' band marching along Maderia Drive on the occasion of the Historic Military Vehicle Run. See also page 61.

East Street (*c*1995): The colourful wheel and mini funfair would not have been allowed in this area 'in the old days' but with the ever-changing character of Brighton, it enhances the vibrancy of the city.

The Great Storm (1987): Beach huts at Hove destroyed by hurricane-force winds. See also pages 64 and 65.

Hare Krishna (2002): The Hare Krishna festival is held in September every year. This year it was held at the Peace Statue on the Brighton and Hove border. In the background is the colourful temple on wheels.

Dieppe Street Market: See also page 71.

The Brighton Tour Bus (2002)**:** The bus departs from Brighton Pier, travels out as far as the Marina and stops at all the main places of interest, and you can get on and off at your leisure.

Hove Lagoon (2002): This attractive mural caught my eye and can be seen from quite a distance away. The entire walled area of the lagoon has been painted in this 'sea' theme.

George Street, Hove (1998): Pedestrianisation and pavement cafés where once there was two-way traffic.

Day-trippers

London barrow boys (*c*1958): They used to push their barrows from London once every summer and sell their fruit and veg on the Palace Pier forecourt for a pensioners' charity. You can't see the barrows because of the crowds.

Fancy a bit of horseplay? (*c*1965): A rather unusual occurrence to see a horse-rider on the forecourt of the Palace Pier! The day-tripper standing by the horse took advantage of the situation to have

this photo taken. The rider's parents had a fish and chip shop in West Street.

Monkeying around! (*c*1956): A visiting monkey prepares to take photographs on the lower promenade at the bottom of West Street. The young boy's 'I don't believe what I'm seeing' expression speaks for itself.

Day-trippers

A modest poser! (*c*1968): This young la
visited Brighton every summer and alwa
asked me to take her photograph on the Pal
Pier forecourt. With two parrots perched
her arms, I'm still not sure whether t
expression is one of happiness or 'help'
think that this photograph personifies
heady days of the 'swinging sixties'; fash
changed dramatically and young won
were given the freedom to earn good mor
and to spend it on what they wanted.

One for the family album (*c*1976)
This group is on the lower promena
between the two piers, enjoying a fun
out.

Day-trippers

A hat roost! (*c*1976): This lady was a frequent visitor to the Palace Pier. She is pictured here with the parrot on the Pier forecourt. I think she was wise to keep her hat on!

Young love (*c*1968): This young couple on the Palace Pier forecourt were enjoying their day out; the young lady was cooling down with an ice cream on a particularly warm day.

Just another happy family (*c*1974): A family enjoying a day out together on the lower promenade between the two piers. I had no difficulty in encouraging people to sit on any of my animal props.

Local residents

Fishermen (*c*1961): During this era it was quite common to see local fishermen pulling in their nets on the beaches.

An exhibitionist (*c*1965): A somewhat extroverted, heavily tattooed young lady, who wanted to adopt this pose on the Palace Pier forecourt! As you can imagine, she attracted a great deal of attention from passers-by and I can honestly say that a photo of this nature happened only on rare occasions.

Local residents

Twins (*c*1959): These twins, right, were cuddled up to one another in their pram on the lower promenade. They were fast asleep, oblivious to what was going on around them. Their parents wanted a photograph to capture this most unusual sleeping position.

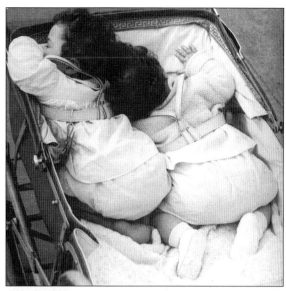

Another set of twins

(*c*1959): These twins, left, were also taken in their pram on the lower promenade. However, they were in a more relaxed position but still fast asleep. Their parents just could not resist having a photograph taken of them in this position.

And another set of twins (1959): The owner of these twin monkeys called me over to a deckchair on the lower promenade where I found them cuddled up. No wonder the owner wanted a photograph for the album.

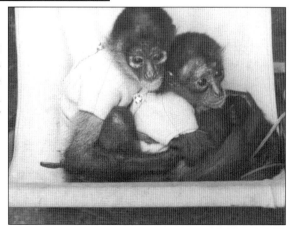

Local residents

A poodle-eye view (*c*1960): This poodle seemed to enjoy visiting the Palace Pier and standing up to view the beach. As I said to its owner, 'Perhaps he's just having a look around for another poodle!'

The poodle poser (*c*1960): This poodle decided to have a good look round on the Palace Pier forecourt for a mate!

Another poser (*c*1965): Even dogs liked to pose on the animal props. I swear this dog deliberately posed for this shot on the Palace Pier forecourt; could that be a smile?

Local residents

Sunshine Joe (*c*1960): Local art students liked Sunshine Joe, as he was nicknamed. He was one of Brighton's best-known characters and had a great sense of humour. He would sit on the beach and draw cartoons on pieces of cardboard and write underneath '£80 or near offer'. Obviously he didn't get anything near that but he did earn enough to buy a pint or two.

Car washers (*c*1964): These two could have been the first car washers in Brighton. They appeared on the Palace Pier forecourt on that well-remembered Bank Holiday when the Mods and Rockers clashed on the Aquarium terrace. They were drawn to the pier because they had heard about the fight and wanted to be in on the action. Their natural habitat was New Road, near the Theatre Royal. They cleaned the cars of unsuspecting theatre patrons and hoped to be rewarded when the owners returned to their cars.

Local residents

A motley crew! (*c*1972): A group of pals sitting outside St Andrew's Church, Church Road, Hove. What were their stories, I wonder?

The bag lady (*c*1965): This woman was a familiar local character in the 1960s. She slept on benches surrounded by her personal belongings packed into several plastic bags. She was pictured here on a bench near the Royal Pavilion. She's now long gone.

Local residents

The Promettes (*c*1957): These six smartly dressed young ladies were called the 'Promettes' and they used to patrol the promenade at weekends directing visitors to places of interest in the town and giving advice on bus and train timetables. The photograph shows them with a visiting dignitary on the upper promenade between the two piers.

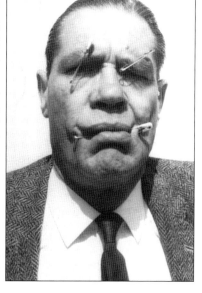

The original pin up! (*c*1960): This was rather an unusual request for this man's photograph to be taken on the Palace Pier forecourt with safety-pins secured to his face.

A winning smile (*c*1968): This extremely photogenic and happy young lady used to come on to the Palace Pier frequently to have her photograph taken.

Local residents

The 'garden' lady (*c* late 1950s–early 1960s): This lady lived in Liverpool until she retired, but then decided to move to Brighton. She liked to have her photograph taken at various parks and gardens in the town. Left, the Royal Pavilion; below, Steine Gardens; bottom, the Sunken Gardens near the Peace statue on the Brighton–Hove border.

Local residents

'Burlington Bertie' (*c*1970-1980): Burlington Bertie (my name for him) was perhaps one of the most extrovert characters I have ever come across. He was a familiar figure along the coast,

especially in the Brighton, Shoreham and Worthing areas. He is seen, right, strolling along the lower promenade at Brighton, and left, enjoying a pint outside the Bridge Hotel at Shoreham. He was also often seen cycling in this attire and would wave to passers-by. Children liked to pursue him.

'The extrovert' (*c*1960): This dapper man, with his trilby and rolled umbrella, was a well-known local extrovert who decided on this occasion to perform an impromptu dance on the Palace Pier forecourt for the benefit of bemused onlookers.

Local residents

Sisters (*c*1976): Many local people were my regular customers and this family was one of them. These sisters, shown with their children, used to seek me out on the seafront to keep up-to-date photographs for their albums.

Heatons Transport (*c*1965): A lorry parked near the Palace Pier defies the laws of gravity; the driver was not amused!

Special events

London to Brighton Veteran Car Run (*c*1995): The first run took place in 1896 to celebrate the Locomotive and Highways Act which removed the requirement for a man with a red flag to walk in front of every automobile. The event, eligible only for cars of 1905 and before, is one of the UK's biggest annual motoring attractions with crowds in excess of one million lining the route. Above, competitors passing Pavilion Gardens, and below, approaching the finishing line in Marine Drive.

Special events

The Milk Race (1965): The first Tour of Britain cycle race (Milk Race) started from Brighton in 1965. Government legislation was introduced in 1960, which legalised cycle road racing and paved the way for such events as the Tour of Britain. The cyclists can be seen lining up in Marine Drive for the start of the race.

London to Brighton walk (*c*1959): Don Thompson is pictured on his way to winning one of his many London to Brighton walks. He's turning the corner from the Aquarium into Marine Drive and is in view of the winning post. Don won the 50km walk Olympic Gold Medal in Rome. He set a new Olympic record for the event of 4:25:30 hours.

Special events

Brighton & Hove Albion FC (1978): Players Brian Horton (left) and Chris Cattlin (right) performing a lap of honour in celebration of the Seagulls' promotion to Division 1.

Below, the Seagulls' manager, Alan Mullery (left), chairman, Mike Bamber (middle) and coach, George Aitken (right) joining in the celebrations.

Above, the famous North Stand at the Goldstone ground, where the hardcore of fans stood.

Right, players Mark Lawrenson and Michael Kerslake.

Special events

Albion promoted again (2002): The Seagulls on the balcony of Brighton & Hove City Council's offices on the Hove seafront celebrating their return to Division 1. See also page 39.

The Brighton and Hove Half Marathon (c1996): The start of the half marathon race sponsored by *The Argus* and Whitbread. The runners set off from the Peace statue on the Brighton and Hove border, went on to Hove Lagoon, turned and made for Rottingdean and then came back for the finish at the Peace statue.

Historic Military Vehicle Run (1996): This London to Brighton run is an annual event and has taken place for more than fifty years. There is a wide variety of vehicles to look at including tanks, jeeps, motorcycles and trucks. Many owners dress in authentic military uniforms.

US Sherman tank, right.

British Scorpion tank, below.

Special events

Girl pipers and dancers (*c*1965): A group of Scottish girl pipers and dancers performing on the forecourt of the West Pier before its sad decline.

Ace Café Reunion (2002): Thousands of bikers descended on Brighton for the annual Ace Café Reunion. It was a highly charged affair. As an onlooker you could sense the wonderfully exhilarating atmosphere of the event caused by the sheer number of bikers, the roar of the engines and the pounding rock music bursting out from the truck.

Left, the arrival of a group of bikers in Maderia Drive.

Opposite, top, the Ace Café Reunion truck.

Special events

The National Windsurfing Championships (*c*1987), held off the beach at the bottom of Hove Street.

The Great Storm

The Great Storm (1987): This fierce storm caused large-scale damage that had not been seen for more than 250 years. There were Force 10 winds with gusts of up to 113mph, causing severe structural damage to houses, fences, roofs, chimney pots etc. Vehicles were overturned and hundred of trees were uprooted.

Left, Holy Trinity Church, Blatchington Road, Hove.

Below, opposite the Royal Pavilion and Dome (scaffolded and sheeted during a restoration programme).

The Great Storm

Wind of Fury

Black clouds drove in from the sea
Trying to blot out the clear blue sky.
The hurricane wind blew free,
White candyfloss clouds hurried by
As if fleeing from a fiend.
Sea birds blown about the sky;
Into the wind a man leaned,
Must try to walk not reason why.
Nature is beautiful but sometimes cruel,
The sun defiant shone through a dark cloud.
Nature does not respect any given rule;
However she behaves, she is proud.
Little ships ran for the shore
Like bats out of hell
Before they were eaten up and were no more.
My God, I wished them well
But we mere mortals to survive
Must often fight to stay alive.

Above, New Road, oppo-
site the Theatre Royal.

Right, Old Steine Gardens.

Changing face of Brighton and Hove

West Pier (*c*1985): The West Pier in the 1980s before it became more dilapidated. The pretty, wild flowers in the foreground almost give it a 'picture post-card' look.

Below (*c*1995), the pier on a stormy winter's day which inspired my poem *The Lonely Pier*. The pier was near total collapse after storms and a fire early in 2003 but a restoration plan has now been accepted in principle and the pier may be restored by 2005.

Changing face of Brighton and Hove

The Lonely Pier

People have walked on me,
People have used me,
People have loved me,
People have abused me.
Now I am discarded,
Stretching out to sea.
Derelict, deserted and lonely,
No more the laughter of children on my deck.
I am just a poor abandoned wreck.
No more the trippers from London town
Sitting in deckchairs, getting brown.
Now only the gulls to keep me company.
Please save me and restore my dignity.

View from the Palace Pier (1999): Looking west towards the West Pier taking in an area of Brighton beach between the two piers (note the towering bungee jump is in view to the right of the West Pier).

Changing face of Brighton and Hove

Bungee jumping (1999): A relatively new pastime for some daredevils but leaping from a high place, secured by a bungee around the ankles, is not my idea of fun! Note the children's paddling pool (now closed but a new one was built in 2000) on the lower promenade and part of the West Pier in the foreground.

Children's playground and paddling pool (2000): A new, colourful development including children's paddling pool situated between the West Pier and the Brighton and Hove border.

Changing face of Brighton and Hove

Brighton Fishing Museum (1995): The museum is situated on the lower promenade close to Brighton Pier. This was the opening day and, as you can see, it brought many people on to the seafront.

Mural (*c*1992): This mural was a beautiful work of art and was purportedly painted by a local art student. It was displayed on the wall of a small shelter near West Street, Brighton, on the lower promenade. It depicted a little of Brighton's history when fishing was the main industry. Unfortunately, the mural was vandalised and has subsequently been painted over.

Changing face of Brighton and Hove

Dieppe Street Market (*c*1995): This popular annual market, when French market traders come over from Dieppe to sell their produce, is held in Bartholomew Square, near The Lanes in Brighton.

The Fountain, Steine Gardens (2002): The building in the middle distance was once used to house public lavatories but has now been converted into an attractive café with outside seating and umbrellas.

Changing face of Brighton and Hove

Buskers: Above (2002), one of the many groups providing entertainment on the lower promenade area, between the two piers. Below (1998), in George Street, Hove.